GW00499009

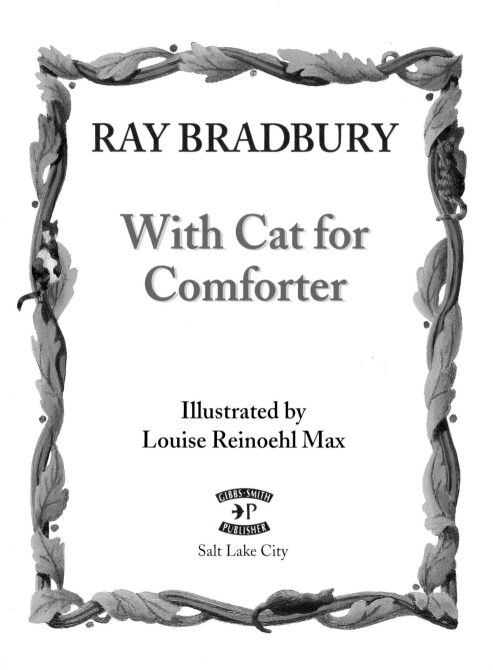

RAY BRADBURY

With Cat for
Comforter

Illustrated by
Louise Reinoehl Max

GIBBS·SMITH
➔P
PUBLISHER

Salt Lake City

First edition
00 99 98 97   5 4 3 2 1

Text copyright © 1997 by Ray Bradbury
Illustrations copyright © 1997 by Louise Reinoehl Max

This is a Peregrine Smith Book, published by
Gibbs Smith, Publisher
P.O. Box 667
Layton, Utah 84041

Design by David Charlsen, San Francisco, CA
Printed and bound in China

Library of Congress Cataloging-in-Publication Data
Bradbury, Ray, 1920–
    With cat for comforter / by Ray Bradbury : illustrated
by Louise Reinoehl Max.
       p.   cm.
    "A Peregrine Smith book"—T.p. verso.
    ISBN 0-87905-752-1
    1. Cats—Poetry. I. Max, Louise Reinoehl, 1954– . II. Title.
PS3503.R167W56   1997
811'.54—dc21   97-8081
                                                                CIP

The genesis of this book was one morning just before dawn six months ago, when I lay slowly waking to the sound of three teakettles simmering. Or, to put it another way, to the hum of a beehive in midsummer. But then, finally, to three cats running their motors at half-throttle. The sound was so pleasantly reassuring that it almost lulled me back to sleep. *Comforting* was the word that entered my head. And then *comforter*—which propelled me out of bed full-tilt to get me to my typewriter before the poem—for that was what it was—melted. Five minutes later, all these lines were done and I headed back to join my cats in their twenty-hour marathon of kip and snooze.

How many cats have there been in my life? Not enough. But a rough figure would be thirty-five or forty, one or two at a time, and then one flabbergasting cluster when our daughters were young.

Back in 1957, upon returning from a visit to Paris with my family, I was greeted by our two pregnant cats, bursting with life. One immediately hid in a closet, the other under the bed. I ran to fetch a flashlight.

During the next hour I leaped back and forth from the bed to the closet, back to the bed, as two, four, six, eight, ten, twelve, thirteen kittens slid forth into a world of laughter. Sometimes we forget, until it returns, our belief in life, no matter how rough. On the nights when our children are born, the celebrations seize us to provoke the cries of joy. I have never known many happier moments of laughter than that night when the mother cats outdid themselves in a litter competition—superseded only, of course, by the anxious but wildly happy nights when our daughters entered the world. By nine in the evening it was all over; the closet was brimmed with six new lives. The bed sheltered the odd number, seven. Exhausted, as if I had done the whole thing, I had a beer— hell, why not *three?*

The final sum was twenty-two cats in one household simultaneously, for the thirteen new ones mingled with nine full-grown, already there!

In the highs and lows of cats and family in later years, one high came when the Purina Cat Chow folks chose to photograph our milk-and-caramel tom Tater, or Ho-Ichi the Earless. He was named for that Japanese ghost hero who was invisible save for his ears, which were soon torn off by his enemies. Tater Ho-Ichi, partially earless, became the Purina Cat Chow October cat. His face appeared in ninety thousand calendars in 1988, several hundred of which we mailed to friends, neighbors, relatives, and people we hardly knew.

The Purina folks further rewarded us with a photo portrait of Tater Ho-Ichi, four feet high and three feet wide, which resides on the stairs leading from the kitchen to our library, where we can see it a dozen times a day. We have yet to light candles at this shrine, but we are considering it.

Tater Ho-Ichi had a dozen other names, like our other cats. I think most of us try names on our loves like shoes, comfortable or uncomfortable, until one truly fits. Marmalade becomes Marmalata becomes, when she fattens, Lotta Marma. Blackie becomes Ditzi when we see her behavior. I am busy writing a new book titled *The Cat With Ten Million Names* and have the cats to prove it.

Finally, and it is hard to get this cat-lover to shut up, there was the experience I had another time in Paris. Invited by the French government to celebrate Jules Verne's birthday, my wife and I attended the Bastille Day military parade in mid-Paris. The next day, a reporter from a far-left radical paper interviewed me.

"Monsieur Bradbury," he said, "do you consider yourself a pacifist?"

"I think so, yes," I replied.

"Then, Monsieur Bradbury," he went on, "how is it that we saw you yesterday in the Champs Elysees grandstand with our president, reviewing the Bastille Day tanks and guns?"

"All of my life," I responded, "I have gone to *dog* shows. And gone home to raise *cats*."

That, dear friends, was the headline in the far-left radical paper the next day. I rest my case.

—Ray Bradbury
March 9, 1997

With cat for comforter,
How still the night.

How right the leaves
That pattern-quilt the bed
And touch a snow pelt on the sill.

How still the air,
While rarer still
And silently aware,
The slumberous cat
That sounds the stillness
With a breath not breath,

The merest inner stir
Of moonlit hive,
Where soul and blood connive
To summon up a mingling of sound
That whispers, listen now:

And now and now
Alive, alive, alive.

Again, again
The rarefied, the ambient,
All quietness in amber caught
And dreamed upon

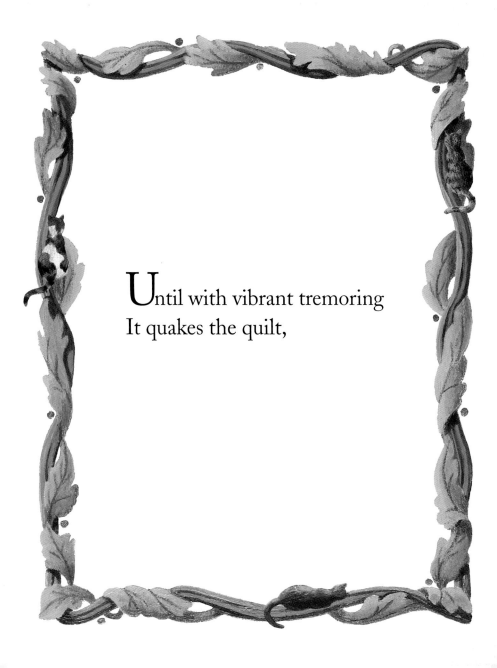

Until with vibrant tremoring
It quakes the quilt,

But inwardly,
With not a breath of outwarding,
But all withheld and susurrant.

You waken to its stir,
Imbedded with its purr,

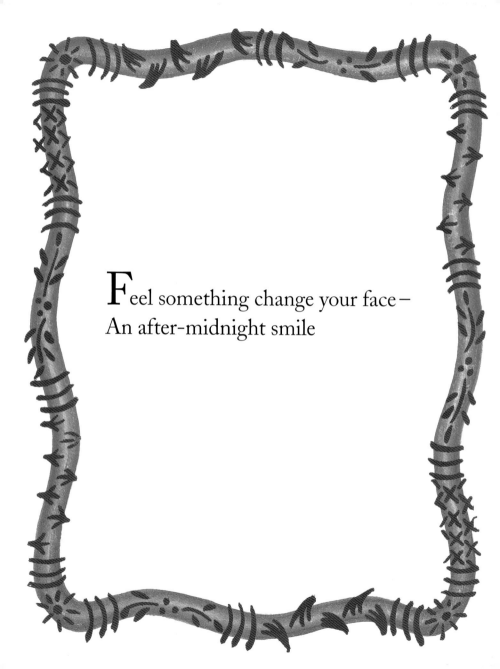

Feel something change your face –
An after-midnight smile

That drifts you slumber-kept
At slept beast's still behest,
His restful sound now yours,
His sound the hearth that cures.

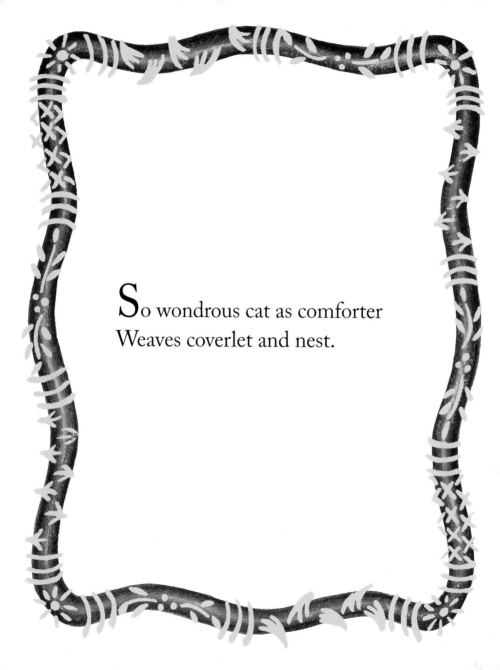

So wondrous cat as comforter
Weaves coverlet and nest.